RAF TODAY

RAF TODAY

ALAN W HALL

Bison Books

Published by
Bison Books Ltd
176 Old Brompton Road
London SW5
England

ISBN 0 86124 313 7

Printed in Hong Kong

Reprinted 1988

The author and publishers would like to thank Richard
Garratt who designed this book. The majority of the
pictures used are Crown copyright, Ministry of Defence and
the publishers would like to thank the staff of the RAF
Recruiting and Photo Library, MoD Rep(S) and MoD
(PE) Farnborough for their help in obtaining these
illustrations. The publishers would also like to thank the
following for supplying pictures.

British Aerospace: pp 1, 19, 22–3, 24–5, 26 (B), 32 (B), 38
(T), 66–7, 69, 70, 87, 88, 88–9, 92, 93.

Austin J Brown/Aviation Picture Library: pp 4–5, 6–7,
17 (T), 18 (T), 20 both, 22 (T), 23, 28 (B), 31 (B), 34–5, 35,
37 both, 38 (B), 45 (T), 71 (B), 76, 77 both, 78 (B), 90 all 3,
91 both, 96

Jeremy Flack/Aviation Photos International: pp 48 (B),
59 (B)

Stuart Howe: p 31 (T)

MAP/Brian Pickering: pp 58, 59 top 3

MARS Lincs: p 26 (T)

Short Bros: pp 94–5

Page 1: Hawk training aircraft.
Nearest the camera is an aircraft in
the standard colours of No. 4 Flying
Training School, RAF Valley. In the
background an aircraft of No. 1
Tactical Weapons Unit and finally a
Hawk in the air defence livery.
Page 2–3: A 29 Squadron Phantom
from RAF Coningsby.
This page: The Hercules remains the
backbone of the RAF transport force.

CONTENTS

The first squadron within Strike Command to become
operational on the Tornado GR.Mk. 1 was No. 9 Squadron
at present based at RAF Honington, Suffolk. ZA596:L
displays the unit's green and yellow bat badge on the fin.

ROYAL AIR FORCE
STRIKE COMMAND

The importance of Strike Command to the present day Royal Air Force cannot be over emphasised. Not only is it the lynch pin of the air defence of the United Kingdom but also controls the RAF's retaliatory air forces elsewhere in the world apart from the squadrons stationed in Germany.

The Command came into being on 30 April 1968, with its headquarters at RAF High Wycombe, Buckinghamshire. The initial move was to merge Fighter and Bomber Commands left over from World War 2 into a single force concentrating on both defensive and offensive forces but in a unified command structure so that operations could be co-ordinated and the wider aspects of defence better considered. Later both Transport and Coastal Commands were destined to merge with Strike Command for the same reasons so that in the present day concept Air Chief Marshal Sir Peter Harding, the AOC-in-C Strike Command, controls all Britain's front line aircraft including fighters, strike/attack, transport, maritime aircraft and the helicopter force throughout the world. RAF Germany is the only exception but both of these Commands are linked through NATO as the post of Commander-in-Chief United Kingdom Air Forces (CINCUKAIR) is combined with the purely RAF appointment.

The mention of NATO and Britain's position within that organisation is worthy of some further study as RAF Strike Command is committed to Allied Command Europe (ACE) but a proportion, notably the maritime squadrons are responsible to the Supreme Allied Commander Atlantic (SACLANT).

A force of this size can best be measured in numbers. RAF Strike Command controls 5,000 civilian employees and 47,000 servicemen and women, in other words nearly half the present strength of the RAF. Some 1,000 aircraft, featuring just over 20 different types, are spread through approximately 200 units of various sizes, the majority, of course, in the United Kingdom.

To control an organisation this size delegation of command is necessary. The overall responsibility rests with RAF Strike Command Headquarters but three Groups within that Command are delegated to deal with their own specialisations. No. 1 Group, with its headquarters at Upavon, Wiltshire, is responsible for strike/attack operations, transport aircraft, air-to-air refuelling and the support of the Army in the field. No. 11 Group corresponds to what was the old Fighter Command. With its headquarters established at Bentley Priory, near London, its previous associations with the Battle of Britain and this important part of the air defence of the United Kingdom are of the utmost importance. All fighter assets of Strike Command are concentrated here and, like most of the other Groups, Bentley Priory has its underground operations room from which any future battle would be fought.

The maritime forces at the disposal of Strike Command come under No. 18 Group. Here co-operation with the Royal Navy is essential and therefore this headquarters is co-located with Fleet Headquarters at Northwood, Middlesex, and takes responsibility not only for anti-submarine and shipping operations but for search and rescue tasks as well. Subsidiary headquarters to No. 18 Group are those at Pitrievie in Scotland and Plymouth, Devon.

Although Strike Command's prime responsibilities are within the United Kingdom and NATO, it also has world-wide commitments in Cyprus, Hong Kong, Belize, the Falklands, Ascension Island and Gibraltar. Detachments are also maintained at various locations in the United States and Canada.

In time of war Britain would become a forward base for reinforcements from the United States and for counter measures against enemy operations in the Atlantic. There is no doubt that the main threat to the United Kingdom would be from air attack to prevent convoys from the

Making the normal fighter-type approach to its base at Coningsby, Lincolnshire, this Phantom of No. 29 Squadron is pictured over the Hardened Aircraft Shelters which now house most operational aircraft within Strike Command. The aircraft itself features contemporary three-tone grey camouflage with low-visibility national and unit insignia.

United States reaching British ports and against airfields which would be active in the defence of these facilities and for launching attacks on a numerically superior enemy.

Defence of British air space is therefore a vital task for Strike Command. In peace time there are three major airfields committed to this role namely those at Leuchars in Scotland, Wattisham, Suffolk and Binbrook, Lincolnshire. Second line bases at Conningsby, Chivenor, Brawdy and Leeming would be activated in case of need but are at the moment engaged either in the training task or are being converted to an operational capability.

The defence fighter force is currently equipped with Phantom and Lightning aircraft with four squadrons of the former dispersed at Leuchars and Wattisham and the Lightnings at Binbrook. The Phantoms have the longer range of the two and are fitted with pulse doppler radar. The Skyflash and Sparrow missiles with which they are armed have the ability to locate and attack targets from above including fast low-flying raiders which are the most difficult to detect by radar when ground-based. As a secondary role the Scottish-based Phantoms are committed to the protection of shipping from air attack and to act as escorts for the Buccaneer force which is also based in Scotland and part of No. 18 Maritime Group.

Another squadron of Phantoms was purchased from surplus US Navy stocks in 1983 to replace the squadron which has been assigned to the air defence role in the Falklands. These F-4Js, modified to British requirements, equip No. 74 Squadron at Wattisham and will remain in service for the foreseeable future.

The Lightning is now becoming obsolescent due to the limitations of its radar equipment and its short range – a characteristic of most post-war developed British fighters. It is planned to start the replacement of these aircraft shortly with the air defence variant of the Tornado. These aircraft have already been delivered to the Operational Conversion Unit (OCU) at Coningsby and should be deployed initially to Leeming when this station has been modified to receive them. Some Phantoms, notably the F.Mk. 1s now based at Leuchars, which were taken over by the RAF when the Royal Navy lost its fixed wing role, will also be among the first to go. Meanwhile the Lightning is by no means outclassed as a fighter. It has the speed necessary for rapid interceptions and retains its fantastic rate of climb but does require constant air-to-air refuelling if taking part in any long-range interceptions.

In time of war the fighter force will be supplemented by the BAe Hawk T.Mk. 1 which at present is in use as an advanced trainer, primarily with Support Command but also as the standard type serving with Strike Command's Tactical Weapons Units at both Brawdy, South Wales and Chivenor, Devon. Most of the Hawks at these bases have been modified to take two AIM-9L Sidewinder infra-red

Below: Lightning F.6 XR755:BF of No. 11 Squadron streams its tail parachute to assist in runway braking after an air combat patrol. The Lightning is now rather obsolescent due to its poor range and outdated Airpass radar but it still has a fantastic rate of climb enabling it to beat almost any other contemporary fighter into the air.

Above: The Queen's Flight will eventually be re-equipped with the BAe 146 and in order to assess its suitability for special duties two of these four-jet civil airliners were given military markings and spent almost a year at RAF Benson for route and role trials. They will be replacing the Andovers at present in service.

guided missiles and with their cannon armament can be expected to add considerably to the effectiveness of the Command's close-in support of bases within the British Isles or in company with a Phantom, using the latter's radar for guidance, for in-depth defence on combat air patrol. Most of the modified Hawks have also been given a new toned-down paint scheme to go with their new role.

Penetrations of British air space by Soviet long-range reconnaissance aircraft are commonplace and since the late 1960s these have been intercepted far out over the Norwegian Sea by British fighters and suitably escorted away from the coast. Penetrations have been made farther south into the North Sea, but the majority of these encounters, which can amount to several each week, have been confined to northern waters.

At each of the three operational fighter bases aircraft are maintained in a constant state of readiness in Quick Reaction Alert shelters 365 days of the year. Working in conjunction with the three main radar sector stations at Buchan, Neatishead and Boulmer or the Shackletons of No. 8 Squadron from Lossiemouth acting as advanced radar pickets, Phantoms or Lightnings can be scrambled within minutes of a target being picked up. A constant game of tactics designed to give away as little as possible of Strike Command's potential is waged almost daily far out to sea and incidentally mostly beyond the knowledge of the British public.

The launching of fighter aircraft is, however, only a small part of the back-up operation needed in their support. Because of the fighters' short range, particularly the Lightning's, a patrol of two must be refuelled in flight during the mission. At the same time as the fighters get airborne from their bases, a tanker aircraft has also to be airborne to support them.

Great consideration has been given to reinforcing the tanker aircraft squadrons since the Falklands war and the realisation of how important these aircraft are to combined operations against intruders. The RAF, up until that time, relied on two squadrons of Handley Page Victor K.2s, converted V-bombers, based at Marham. The emergency measures taken during the Falklands operations involved the conversion of a number of semi-retired Vulcan B.2s and Hercules transport aircraft to the tanker role to supplement the Victors on the long flight from Ascension Island to the South Atlantic.

At that time the RAF had acquired a number of ex-airline operated VC-10s and these have now been converted for use by No. 101 Squadron at Brize Norton in the tanker role. More recently surplus Lockheed TriStars were bought from British Airways and these are currently being rebuilt by Marshalls at Cambridge into long-range tankers and cargo aircraft which will provide the RAF with better facilities in the future. Six TriStars are in the process of conversion for operation by No. 216 Squadron. Both the VC-10 and TriStar have retained part of their freight or passenger capability so that in emergency they can be used not only to refuel operational aircraft en-route to a trouble spot but also carry the maintenance crews so essential in keeping air defence or strike aircraft operational during an extended deployment.

Ground defence of the strategically vital airfields of Strike Command is entrusted to two basic missile systems. The Bloodhound ground-to-air missile of the sixties is still operational in the United Kingdom. These were withdrawn from RAF Germany and now are deployed in a number of locations which provide area defence for key installations and are likely to remain effective in this role, due to updating of their capabilities with better acquisition radar and more sophisticated anti-detection systems.

Close-in airfield defence is maintained by the RAF Regiment and the BAe Rapier short-range missile which, incidentally has also been purchased by US forces stationed in Britain. These missiles are an extremely capable form of defence against low-flying enemy aircraft and are deployed around airfields in quantity. They can be operated with or without radar guidance in the case of the enemy using radar supression measures and are one of the most advanced and effective means of local defence against strike aircraft that have penetrated other·forms of airborne defence.

Additionally a programme of providing Hardened Aircraft Shelters (HAS) is now all but complete in the United Kingdom. These specially equipped concrete shelters, which provide protection against all but a direct hit, are self-contained as far as the aircraft inside are concerned. Fuel, armament and associated services can all be provided and all that is needed to be done is the

---

Below: In-flight refuelling is essential to most operational flights undertaken by Strike Command aircraft. Precision flying is necessary to hook-up to the tanker, in this case a Victor K.2 of No. 57 Squadron. The aircraft receiving fuel is a Phantom from RAF Coningsby.

opening of the massive steel doors and a fully operational fighter can be launched in a matter of seconds.

Elsewhere on these important air defence airfields measures have been taken to protect operations rooms and essential fuel dumps and the personnel to man them. The airfields themselves have been toned down and camouflaged as far as possible.

Precautions have also been taken to protect the vital runways needed to launch and recover aircraft. Modern weapons have been developed by both the Allied and Soviet sides which can easily crater runways using small bomblets thus rendering non-effective all other means of counter measures if aircraft cannot be got into the air. At each of the bases concerned the Army's Royal Engineers have large reserves of runway repair equipment consisting of flexible steel matting which can be quickly laid allowing runways and taxiways to become usable again shortly after an attack.

With the phasing out of Britain's 'V'-force Vulcans and the re-equipment of three squadrons with Tornado GR.Mk.1s, Strike Command has up-dated its strike/attack force in a quantum leap almost unprecedented under peace-time circumstances. Nos. 9 (at Honington), 27 and 617 Squadrons now based at Marham are superior to any other similar type of unit in service anywhere in the world at the present time.

This was proved in October 1985 when representative aircraft from No. 27 Squadron with a backing of aircraft from the tanker force won, for the second year in succession, the coveted United States Air Force bombing competition against the very best crews which the vastly larger USAF could pit against them. At both high and low-level the Tornado's sophisticated on board systems proved better than the very best that the Americans had available.

Following the theme mentioned earlier of Britain being a strategic base from which support can be provided to the Allied Command Europe, squadrons based at UK airfields are held specifically for the support of either of NATO's flanks. Exercises are frequently held in the freezing conditions of northern Norway or the semitropical conditions encountered in the Mediterranean.

Tactical support of the Army in the field is the responsibility of Strike Command's Harrier and Jaguar assets based at Coltishall and Wittering. The two squadrons of Buccaneers, Nos. 12 and 208, based at Lossiemouth provide a maritime strike capability and use as their main armament the now obsolescent Martel TV-guided weapon or the more sophisticated Sea Eagle.

No. 1 Squadron's Harriers at Wittering, backed up by additional aircraft from No. 233 OCU also based there, frequently deploy into the field and from their hides in wooded countryside close to the battle area use the VTOL characteristics of the Harrier for close support of Army operations. It was No. 1 Squadron that also provided the bulk of the RAF aircraft which went with the Royal Navy on board the carriers *Invincible* and *Hermes* during the Falklands war thus gaining valuable experience for their crews.

From the beginning of November 1984 to early December 1985 two RAF Hercules from the Lyneham Wing were on permanent detachment in Ethiopia moving essential foodstuffs and medical supplies to help famine relief in that country. Operation Bushel, as it was known, moved 30,700 tonnes of grain in 3,594 sorties during that time.

Three squadrons of Jaguars are UK-based at Coltishall, Norfolk. Two of these are devoted to the strike role while the other, No. 41, specialises in photo-reconnaissance work.

No one can deny that the busiest and most committed part of Strike Command in terms of hours and miles flown are the four C-130 Hercules squadrons based at Lyneham in Wiltshire. Wherever there is a crisis, earthquake or famine anywhere in the world these squadrons provide either an immediate airlift or dedicate two or three aircraft to assist local organisations in moving essential supplies into the stricken area.

On top of this their full-time task of providing the Army's logistic support anywhere in the world, including the regular supply flights to Belize and the Falklands, plus the many exercise commitments they are called upon to fly, makes many a difficult problem for the planners, particularly so because RAF servicing schedules always require several of the aircraft to be in the Lyneham hangars undergoing their regular checks.

In the last two years 29 out of the 63 aircraft available have been undergoing a major facelift in that their fuselage length has been increased to accommodate more

cargo capacity and consequently two and sometimes three aircraft at a time have been off line at Marshall's, Cambridge, where this work has been done. Others have been converted to the tanker role. In spite of this the Lyneham Wing's Hercules have never missed a schedule or failed to answer a call for help. This is a remarkable achievement and one which few members of the public realise is going on.

The helicopter force is equally committed and at one time in 1984 the Operational Conversion Unit at Odiham, Hants was planning to move on a temporary basis to Akrotiri, Cyprus in order to take advantage of the better weather in order to get new crews trained on the Chinook because there were no spare aircraft available at home and those already committed to the United Nations peace keeping force in Beirut, and stationed in Cyprus, could be utilised for this purpose.

No. 7 Squadron with Chinooks, and No. 33 Squadron with Pumas, occupy Odiham alongside the OCU. Like their fixed-wing colleagues they are almost always either on exercise or tasked with specialist operations in aid of the civil power. Because of the loss of several Chinooks during the Falklands war it became necessary to order more of this type from the United States. These aircraft have now been delivered and the heavy lift element of Strike Command's helicopter force improved.

Strike Command's helicopter force is not confined to transport duties, however, as an important part of the duties of No. 18 Group, normally responsible for maritime operations, is the search and rescue task which falls mainly on two squadrons, Nos. 22 and 202, which have their headquarters at Finningley, Yorkshire but have operational detachments at nine strategically placed airfields around Britain's coasts. The aircraft used are Wessex (No. 22 Sqdn) and Sea Kings (No. 202 Sqdn) and their main task is providing a rescue service for aircrew who are forced to parachute to safety.

But these aircraft also have a commitment to assist in civil rescues and the bright yellow helicopters are well known to bathers on Britain's beaches during the summer months. Rescues from stranded ships, storm battered yachts, children swept out to sea by the tide, mountaineers and others lost in desolate countryside are all part of the daily work of the SAR force.

The main strength of No. 18 Group, however, is based on the four squadrons of Nimrod MR.2s which are responsible for the protection of shipping lanes and for watching over the activities of Soviet warships in peacetime.

Constant patrols over the Atlantic are maintained and with the update of the Nimrod's sensor devices, which

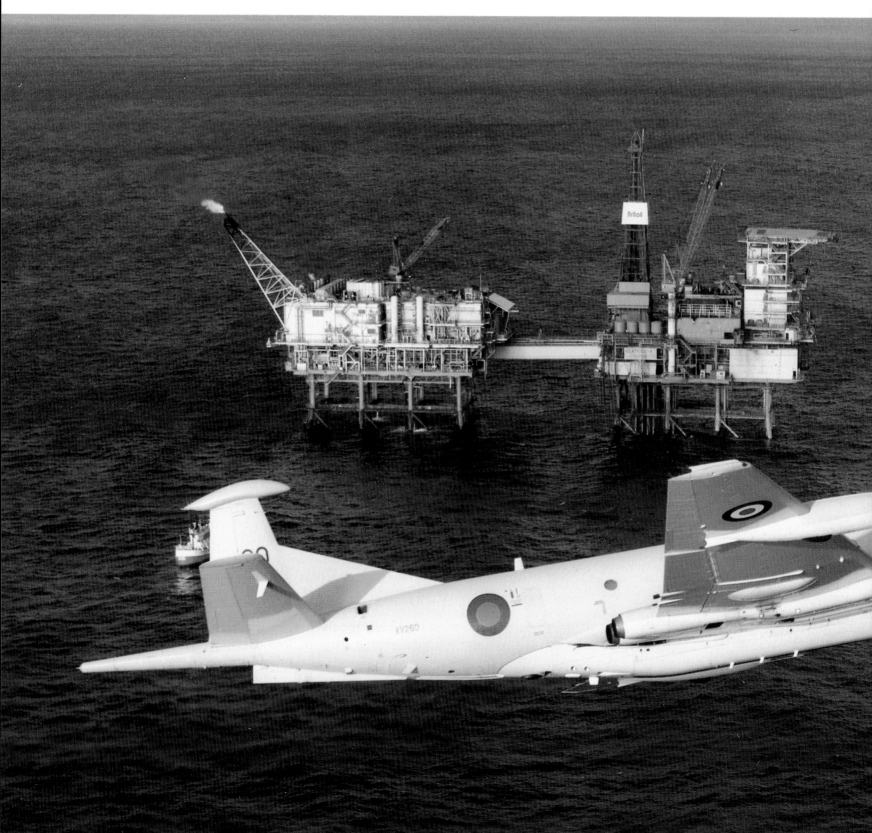

has recently been completed, these aircraft are now one of the most potent of NATO's available aircraft in the event of any war at sea.

They can be armed with either the new Stingray anti-submarine torpedo, depth charges or the American Harpoon air-to-surface missile.

A review of Strike Command is not complete without mention of the various ancillary units that go to make up this powerful and self-contained force. Overseas bases at Hong Kong, Gibraltar, Belize, Cyprus, Sardinia, and of course the Falklands all come under the operational command of High Wycombe. Better known are the Harriers, Phantoms, Hercules, and Chinooks in the Falklands but the Harriers and Pumas in Belize are also doing a valuable

Above: An Air Electronics Operator on board a Nimrod prepares a sonobuoy for launching during an anti-submarine patrol.
Left: Nimrod XV260 was originally built as an MR.Mk. 1 but was included in the up-dating of the maritime force by the installation of far superior electronic equipment and in some cases, in-flight refuelling. Now designated as an MR.Mk. 2P the aircraft belongs to the Kinloss Wing and is seen keeping a watch on a Britoil oil production platform in the North Sea as part of its secondary duties.

peace keeping job. In both Hong Kong and Cyprus there is a squadron of Wessex helicopters, the former engaged on border guardian duties whilst in Cyprus No. 84 Squadron provides air sea rescue facilities for the armament practice camp Phantoms that are on regular detachment at Akrotiri and also provides the helicopter element assisting United Nations forces in keeping the Cypriot peace.

Decimomannu in Sardinia is a similar armament practice camp but this is a NATO one and a small RAF detachment is maintained there to look after the needs of RAF Germany squadrons using the facilities. Gibraltar acts as a staging post and has no squadrons permanently based there.

At home the base of the RAF's last remaining Canberras is Wyton, Cambridgeshire. Here Nos. 100 and 360 Squadrons provide training facilities as targets for exercises or training radar operators. Nimrods and an Andover of No. 51 Sqdn are involved in strategic reconnaissance and the Photographic Reconnaissance Unit has Canberras to develop and apply new techniques in this important role.

RAF Northolt close to London, also has a unique task. It is the base for No. 32 Squadron which operates the RAF's VIP transport squadron of BAe 125s, two Andovers and some Gazelle helicopters. The airfield also hosts most foreign military aircraft up to a certain size having business in the area.

Above: A Tornado F.Mk. 2 of No. 229 OCU Coningsby. The first aircraft of this type, designated to replace Lightnings and some Phantoms in No. 11 Group, Strike Command were delivered to Coningsby in late 1984.

Right: Inside its Hardened Aircraft Shelter at RAF Marham Tornado GR.1 ZA606 of No. 617 Squadron undergoes minor servicing. These shelters are fully equipped with weapons and fuel for quick operational turn-rounds of aircraft and at the same time render the aircraft impervious to attack by all but a direct hit. The external power line for starting the RB.199 engines and all on-board systems is plugged in at all times.

Left: A nine aircraft formation consisting of Tornado GR.Mk. 1s from Nos. 9 and 27 Squadrons practise their low-level formation keeping in preparation for the Queen's birthday flypast over central London during 1984.

Above: A Tornado GR.1 of the Trinational Tornado Training Establishment at Cottesmore, Leicestershire. This unique unit is staffed by the three NATO nations, West Germany, Italy and the United Kingdom, which formed the original manufacturing organisation, Panavia, to build the aircraft. All three contribute instructors to convert pilots onto the aircraft at TTTE, subsequent operational training being undertaken in their respective countries.

Left: The Air Defence Variant of the Tornado is exclusive to the UK within NATO though it has been exported to two Middle East air forces.

Right: Tornado F.2 ZA283, one of three pre-production aircraft, displays its armament of four Sky Flash and two Sidewinder missiles as well as two drop tanks for the photographer on board an RAF Hercules.

Phantoms. Three of the Royal Air Force's most famous squadrons are represented on these two pages.

Left: XV571:A of No. 43 Squadron, known as the 'Fighting Cocks' by the marking on the tail, has been a fighter unit since its inception and spent most of the last war in the Middle East and Italy. It has since been first a Hunter then a Lightning unit but has now had Phantoms since 1969.

Top left: Phantom XT901:Y of No. 56 Squadron, 'The Firebirds', is based at Wattisham and displays an unusual shark's mouth decoration on the nose. No. 56 was formed in June 1916 and flew SE.5As on the Western Front. It was reformed at Hawkinge in 1922 and by the Battle of Britain was flying Hurricanes. Spitfires and Tempests followed before the end of the war and it has since had Meteors, Hunters and Lightnings.

Above: No. 111 Squadron was originally formed in Palestine in World War I and spent much of World War II in service in the Mediterranean. Afterwards it became the RAF's much publicised aerobatic team, the 'Black Arrows' and is now based at Leuchars flying the Phantom FG.1 such as this example XV591:M. which displays a full load of four Sidewinder and four Sparrow missiles for the camera.

Above: Lightning F.6 XR773:DF of the Lightning Training Flight based at Binbrook alongside the two operational Lightning squadrons and used to provide limited conversion training for new pilots coming onto Lightnings for the first time.

Top left: Royal wings . . . This Andover CC.2 is one of five aircraft of this type that are available for use by the Queen's Flight based at RAF Benson, Oxfordshire. Each aircraft is kept in absolutely immaculate condition and regularly used by the Royal family for journeys in this country and abroad. In addition to the Andovers the Queen's Flight has several Westland Wessex helicopters for short journeys. Trials have also been carried out with two BAe 146s with which it is expected the Royal Flight will be equipped by the end of 1986. These will provide the additional range and comfort of a more modern aircraft for the Flight and establish prestige for British Aerospace for their four-jet airliner.

Left: Two Buccaneer S.2Bs of No. 208 Squadron from RAF Lossiemouth fly low over the water close to the mountainous coastline of north-west Scotland exercising their role of maritime strike. This and No. 12 Squadron, also at Lossiemouth, are part of No. 18 Group and are normally armed with either the obsolescent Martel or the new Sea Eagle surface skimming anti-shipping missiles.

Although designed as an advanced trainer the BAe Hawk has reversed the trend, hitherto common, in that an operational fighter at the end of its days normally became used for training purposes. This picture of Hawk XX221 shows the Mk. 1A version which has been adapted to carry two AIM-9L Sidewinder air-to-air missiles for use in area defence during time of war.

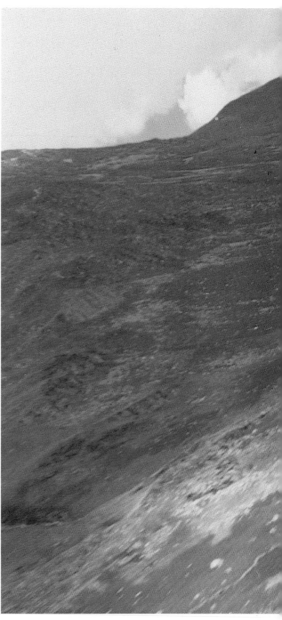

The Strike Command Jaguar force consists of three squadrons based at RAF Coltishall, Norfolk. Out of these Nos. 6 and 54 Squadrons (*above and left, respectively*) are tasked with strike/attack duties while No. 41 Squadron is responsible for photo-reconnaissance work. The Jaguar, an Anglo-French design, remains on active service in the UK whereas RAF Germany has now all but completed the replacement of its Jaguar squadrons with the Tornado. The aircraft remains a vital part of Strike Command's retaliatory strength and the need to keep in constant practice in low-level flight is shown in these pictures. No. 41 Squadron's role is shown in the picture (*right*) in which two groundcrew are seen removing film cassettes from the Jaguar's ventral reconnaissance pack. *Top left*: A Rapier missile unit of No. 66 Squadron, RAF Regiment, pictured at RAF Bentwaters during the home defence exercise 'Brave Defender' in September 1985.

Above: The Harrier GR.Mk. 3 has been in RAF service since the early seventies and is now as useful in the close battlefield support role as ever it was. It is due to be superseded in 1987 by the GR.Mk. 5 version, which has been developed jointly with McDonnell-Douglas in the United States. The aircraft shown here belongs to the only Harrier squadron based in the UK, No. 1, from RAF Wittering. It has a versatile armament but in this view shows four SNEB rocket packs under the wings plus the two centre-line mounted 30-mm Aden cannon.

Left: The two-seat trainer version of the Harrier, the T.Mk. 4, is used by No. 233 OCU also at Wittering.

The Shackleton AEW.2 is the RAF's last remaining operational piston-engined aircraft and is used for radar early warning at low-level to extend the coverage provided by shore-based UK air defence radars. Six Shackletons remain with No. 8 Squadron at RAF Lossiemouth and although they will eventually be replaced by the Nimrod AEW.3, their limited capabilities are used skilfully in the difficult task of intercepting the numbers of Soviet aircraft intrusions into the UK air defence area. All are over 30 years old but they are maintained in immaculate condition.

Right: The Shackleton's rather noisy interior contains two AEW radar operators, a route navigator, engineer and two pilots. The navigator's position is nearest the camera. The engineer is on the right. Shackleton sorties can be anything over ten hours in duration and the noise and turbulence, due to flying at low level over the sea, can be very fatiguing.

Above: The progressive updating of the Nimrod with advanced avionics equipment began in 1977. All four squadrons based at either St. Mawgan, Cornwall, or Kinloss, Scotland have now had this work completed and their aircraft redesignated as Nimrod MR.2s. Among these some have been fitted with in-flight refuelling probes and designated MR.2P as can be seen in this Kinloss Wing aircraft, XV260. Additionally the Nimrod's colour scheme has been changed from light aircraft grey and white to hemp for better camouflage in its working environment. During the Falklands war a number of Nimrods were modified to take underwing Sidewinder missiles in order to provide limited defence against enemy aircraft.

Top right: Canberras of No. 100 Squadron are used for target facilities work either towing air-to-air drogues or as fast low-flying intruders during exercises. This example, WP515, is an original B.Mk. 2 and thought to be one of the oldest Canberras still flying.

Right: Another elderly aircraft which still remains in RAF service is the Hunter T. Mk. 7. Both Nos. 12 and 208 Squadrons of Buccaneers at Lossiemouth have several which are normally used for crew conversion work and routine check flights.

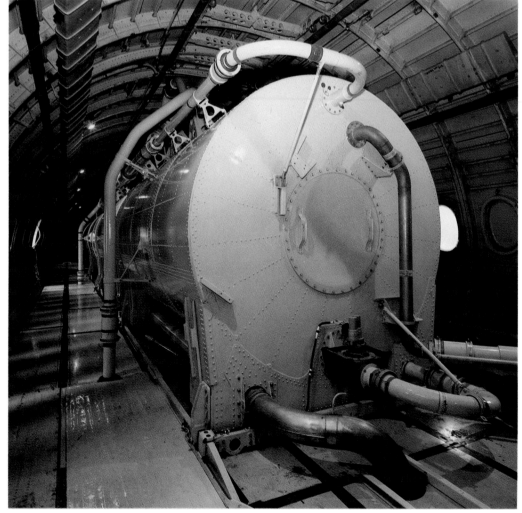

Above : The Victor in-flight refuelling aircraft has done yeoman service over the last decade since the first K.2 was delivered to RAF Marham in May 1974. This picture illustrates the global task undertaken by the 27 B.2s modified for the role in that it was taken at Goose Bay, Labrador, when the aircraft, from No. 55 Squadron, was escorting other Strike Command aircraft on deployment to the United States.

Left : The advent of the VC-10 as a tanker aircraft has greatly enhanced Strike Command's tanker force as its capacity for on-board fuel is twice that of the Victor. This interior view of the aircraft's tanking facility does not show the additional passenger accommodation forward which allows ground crews to accompany both the tanker and the aircraft it is escorting on long-range missions.

Right : The workhorse of Strike Command. Hercules XV192 is one of six from the Lyneham Wing converted to tanker duties. These are stationed at either Ascension Island or in the Falklands to provide in-flight refuelling facilities for the aircraft en route from the UK or short-range air defence aircraft such as Harriers and Phantoms stationed in the Falklands.

Right: One of the six Hercules C.1Ks modified to the in-flight refuelling role and part of No. 1312 Flight based in the Falkland Islands. XV213, seen here, is trailing its single refuelling drogue from the lowered cargo ramp in the rear of the aircraft. Although an interim measure because of the shortage of tanker aircraft during and since the Falklands war, the Hercules has proved an invaluable asset to Falklands operations as with only one airfield available, and sudden weather changes very possible, it has been essential that emergency refuelling facilities have been available.

Below: In its almost desperate attempts to improve the in-flight refuelling facilities available, the Ministry of Defence sought other aircraft that could be readily converted to the role. In addition to the VC-10s of No. 101 Squadron they acquired six former British Airways Lockheed TriStars that are being converted to combined transport and in-flight tanker aircraft. Due to the urgency involved the original aircraft including ZD948, shown here, had their British Airways markings painted out, RAF roundels and serials applied and rushed into service.

Right: The definitive colour scheme and configuration of the RAF's recently acquired TriStar KC.Mk. 1s is shown in this picture of ZD950. Fitted with its own in-flight refuelling probe and with a large cargo door added, it is now operated by No. 216 Squadron from Brize Norton.

Right: The RAF's principal strategic transport aircraft is the VC-10. Fourteen of these aircraft entered service in 1967 with No. 10 Squadron at Brize Norton and since then have flown thousands of servicemen and their dependants to various parts of the world. Apart from maintaining regular scheduled services to overseas bases the squadron has an important freight facility which involves the rapid conversion of the aircraft's interior. This is the responsibility of the versatile Movements Squadrons, including an RAuxAF unit, who rapidly convert the aircraft into a freighter or a medevac configuration in response to demand. A large freight door in the forward fuselage allows for very rapid loading of vehicles such as this Land Rover, aircraft engines or other essential supplies.

Below: The VC-10 has also become part of the Strike Command tanker force. Here ZA140:A of No. 101 Squadron deploys its three in-flight refuelling drogues ready to receive shorter-range aircraft. Nine VC-10 K.2s have been completed but these will be followed by four more VC-10 K.3s which have been converted from the Super VC-10 in civil airline service and which will provide additional fuel facilities and passenger accommodation. Each VC-10 tanker has been given the standard colour scheme of the tanker force, namely hemp, on all upper surfaces with light aircraft grey undersides.

Above: All of the VC-10s of No. 10 Squadron have been given names. Seen on the approach to Brize Norton, its home base, XR808 is named 'Kenneth Campbell VC', in common with all other VC-10s on strength, after famous Victoria Cross holders in the Royal Air Force.

Right: The VC-10 K.2 has four Rolls Royce Conway engines which give a cruising speed in the region of 500 mph. This allows fighter and strike aircraft to make their refuelling contacts well within the flight envelope and at altitude. The aircraft in this picture, ZA143:D is seen at Brize Norton, its home base in Oxfordshire.

Above: The Andover C.1 once the medium-range transport in the RAF has now had a change of role in that the few remaining, after the majority were sold to the Royal New Zealand Air Force, are employed on calibration duties with No. 115 Squadron. This role involves the checking of both airfield, en route navigation and blind landing equipment and requires some very meticulous and accurate flying. No. 115 Squadron, based at RAF Benson has eight Andovers and a secondary role in wartime of casualty evacuation.

Left: One of the other remaining Andovers in RAF service XS606 is used by the Empire Test Pilot's School, Boscombe Down. For performance assessment it has a long probe mounted on the nose and is used by students for test analysis exercises during the year-long course.

This interesting picture shows several aspects of Strike Command's activities. Taken at RAF Neatishead one of the air defence radar sites dominated by the sophisticated radar head, it also has one of the unit's emergency fire tenders in the foreground. Overhead one of No. 202 Squadron's Sea King HAR.3s in its distinctive all-yellow colour scheme hovers while the crewman in the rear doorway instructs the pilot on ground clearance before landing.

The Sea King HAR.3s of No. 202 Squadron are used for air-sea rescue. With their headquarters at Finningley the Sea Kings operate in three separate Flights at Boulmer, Brawdy and Lossiemouth. Each detachment normally has three aircraft available with one always on immediate readiness.

The Royal Air Force Regiment Colour Squadron rightfully claims to be one of the smartest ceremonial drill units in Britain's armed forces. Based at RAF Uxbridge, the squadron specialises in continuity drill movements without a word of command and is a firm favourite at the Royal Tournament and other major displays each year. But apart from displays it has the important task on occasion of mounting guard at Buckingham Palace, the other Royal residences and the Tower of London. Competition between airmen of the RAF Regiment for selection as a member of the squadron is intense as they are all drawn from the ranks and have normal trade specialisations such as drivers, gunners or members of Rapier missile teams. The picture *left* was taken outside Buckingham Palace when the Colour Squadron was taking over guard duties from the Coldstream Guards. In the picture *below* the Colour Guard is seen entering the gates of Buckingham Palace at the start of their tour of duty in London.

Above: The RAF's parachute display team, the Falcons, has 12 members from the instructional team at No. 1 Parachute Training School, Brize Norton. They are frequently seen at air shows in Britain during the summer months and excel in formation free fall manoeuvres such as this 12-man link-up while dropping from a Hercules about two miles above their Oxfordshire base. Each man is a member of the Physical Education Branch and the team was first established in 1965.
Right: An army, or for that matter air force, marches on its stomach, so they say and this is especially true when in the field on exercises where extremes of temperature and working conditions can demoralise an efficient fighting force in a short while unless basic comforts such as a hot meal and dry bedding are available. The RAF prides itself in being able to produce as good a meal in the open as can be done indoors. There's always variety and plenty of it.

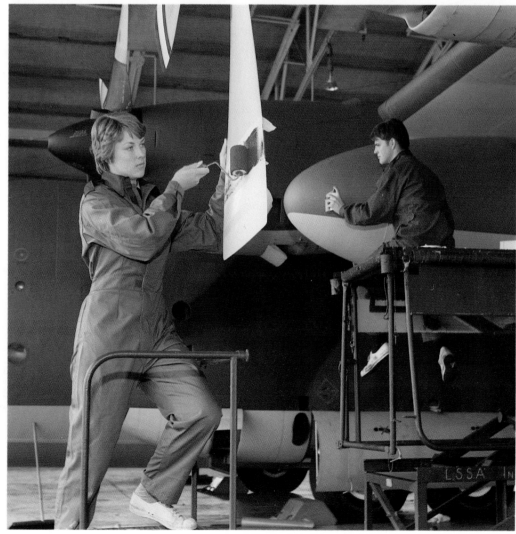

Above: The Harrier has been the aircraft type used by No. 233 Operational Conversion Unit since it was formed at RAF Wittering in 1970. This picture illustrates the unit's badge that appears on the aircraft's nose.

Top left: An RAF Service Policeman with a guard dog, specially trained in anti-intruder operations, patrols one of the Bloodhound ground-to-air missile sites at RAF West Raynham.

Bottom left: Four RAF Puma helicopters and a number of Harrier ground attack aircraft are stationed at Belize in the Carribean as a deterrent to neighbouring countries wishing to invade the former British colony. No. 1563 Flight, as it is known, is supplied by air from the United Kingdom and the Pumas are used to relieve Army outposts on the Belize borders that cannot be reached by road. The dense tropical jungles and the difficulties that might arise from a forced landing are constantly present.

Right: Aircraft maintenance is not only a man's job. Members of the WRAF work alongside their male companions in keeping aircraft on the top line as can be seen in this picture taken in the deep servicing hangar at Lyneham, Wilts, where finishing touches are being put to an RAF Hercules before it goes back on route flying.

45

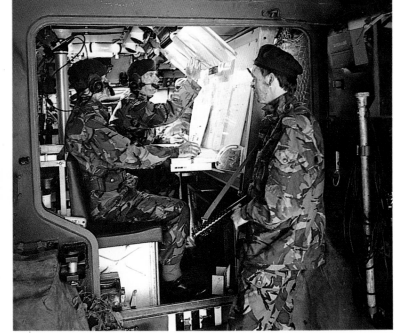

Left: Members of an RAF Regiment Field Squadron disembark from their Spartan Armoured Personel Carrier during an exercise at RAF Wittering. The Regiment is responsible for airfield defence both in an anti-aircraft role and in more conventional infantry deployments against sabotage and terrorist infiltration should the need arise. They are equipped with light armoured fighting vehicles such as the Scorpion and APCs to give the required rapid mobility in the event of an attack. Infantry weapons, mortars and anti-tank missiles are carried. At present there are 15 RAF Regiment Field Squadrons deployed in the UK and RAF Germany.

Below: Often overlooked in the Strike Command hierarchy is the Military Air Traffic Operations (MATO) which exists to co-ordinate military and civil aircraft movements over the confined UK air space. This young lady pictured in the London Air Traffic Control Centre, West Drayton, is tasked with slotting high and low-level military flights through the complicated mass of UK airways and provides emergency facilities should any military aircraft get into difficulties.

Far left: Members of the RAF Regiment also man the low-level airfield defence Rapier missile sites dispersed near to important targets such as airfields and radar sites. This picture shows the visual sighting unit in use though most Rapiers are now equipped with Blindfire radar tracking.

Left: Communications are essential in time of war and each RAF Regiment Field Squadron uses a Sultan Armoured Command Vehicle for this purpose. Radio links between small units, the command vehicle and the Station Operations Room are maintained.

Top left: The RAF Marine Craft Unit was part of No. 18 Group with headquarters at RAF Mountbatten, Plymouth. It was disbanded early in 1986. Before that the MCU maintained a target towing, search and rescue and range safety role for many years since before World War 2. Shown here is HMAFV *Wellington*, a range target towing launch with a top speed of 23 knots and an overall length of 24 metres.

Bottom left: No. 84 Squadron has a dual role apart from being the only resident RAF squadron based at Akrotiri, Cyprus. Apart from its air-sea rescue role in support of the operational squadrons visiting the Sovereign Base Area for armament practice camps, part of the squadron is assigned to United Nations peace keeping duties signified by the light blue band round the rear fuselage of XS498 seen here.

Above: A somewhat unusual view of a Spartan APC seen from the interior of a Chinook helicopter at approximately 1,000 feet over the M27 near Portsmouth. Weighing 8,172 kgs the load is suspended on a single strop from the aircraft's loading beams.

ROYAL AIR FORCE
GERMANY

With the ending of World War 2 and RAF and USAAF air forces occupying the former Luftwaffe airfields the possibility of a new German air force was something on which no one would have taken a bet. But 40 years later the present day West German air forces are of the utmost importance to the defence of Western Europe. The reason why such an important air force can exist and why both British and American air forces still occupy German airfields is all part of the North Atlantic Treaty Organisation story.

Both the United States Air Force and the Royal Air Force maintain bases in Germany under NATO requirements but, apart from certain squadrons, remain under direct operational orders of their respective governments during peace time.

A somewhat complicated chain of command has arisen because of the various national political commitments to NATO but in time of war this would be greatly streamlined. Supreme Headquarters Allied Powers Europe (SHAPE) is at Mons, Belgium, and is always commanded by an American general. This organisation has overall responsibility for NATO forces from the north of Norway to the Russo-Turkish borders but Europe itself comes under Headquarters Allied Forces Europe (AFCENT) with headquarters at Brunsum. Stemming from this headquarters is the air element known as Headquarters Allied Air Forces Central Europe (AAFCE) which has two subordinate commands covering the central region namely the 2nd Allied Tactical Air Force in the north and the 4th Allied Tactical Air Force covering most of southern Germany. The Royal Air Force in time of war would come directly under the command of 2 ATAF together with the air forces of Belgium, the Netherlands and parts of the West German air force.

The area of responsibility of 2 ATAF extends from the Danish border in the north, includes all of Holland and Belgium in the west and the West German border in the east. The southern extremity runs along the northern Luxembourg border and then in a line running north east to Kassel and Gottingen.

With the exception of the two air defence Phantom squadrons based at RAF Wildenrath, which are permanently committed to NATO, the remainder of RAF squadrons based in Germany come under the command of the AOC-in-C RAF Germany with headquarters at Rheindahlen to the west of the Ruhr and close to the Dutch-German border. In time of war this officer would also take over the responsibility of AOC 2 ATAF as a senior NATO commander and all assets of RAF Germany would be fully committed to NATO command. The headquarters would also move to a more secure operations

Previous page: Symbol of present day RAF air power in Germany is the Tornado GR.1. A sophisticated and highly powerful weapon system, these aircraft have replaced the Buccaneer and Jaguar strike aircraft over the last three years following the arrival of the first Tornado for No. VX Squadron in 1983. Now six squadrons based at Bruggen and Laarbruch are working up to their full potential alongside other Tornado squadrons of the West German Air Force in 2 ATAF. A 16 Squadron aircraft is shown.
Right: The art of camouflage is something that the RAF Germany Harrier force fully understands. This two-seat Harrier T.4 hidden in the edge of a wood has additional camouflage nets to form its hide but these can be very quickly swung aside and the aircraft, fully armed, can be on its way to attack a ground target in a matter of minutes. Strips of light metal cladding are used to support the Harrier's undercarriage while inside and moving out of its hiding place.

centre just over the border in Holland as Rheindahlen is the headquarters for the British Army of the Rhine (BAOR) and the Northern Army Group and the present RAF accomodation would be needed.

Four airfields at Wildenrath, Bruggen, Laarbruch and Gutersloh make up the RAF contingent and on them the operational squadrons are based. RAF Germany also has responsibility for RAF Gatow in Berlin but here only transport aircraft operate and a small flight of Chipmunks maintains a token right of occupancy.

The four airfields are known locally as the 'Clutch' and are the base for 14 different RAF squadrons nowadays, mostly made up of Tornado GR.1 strike aircraft, but also including the Harriers of Nos. 3 and 4 Squadrons and the helicopters of Nos. 18 and 230 Squadrons. No. 2 Squadron has photo-reconnaissance Jaguars, Nos. 19 and 92 Squad-

Above: Typical scene during an in-the-field exercise. The pilot signs the Harrier's Form 700 serviceability sheet while ground crew, all in camouflage clothing, and in some cases carrying their individual weapons with them, assist.

rons have Phantoms and the remaining squadron, No. 60 at Wildenrath is responsible for command communications with Pembrokes.

Additionally there is a large RAF hospital at Wegberg and a winter survival school at Bad Kohlgrub in southern Germany. RAF Germany has control of a bombing range at Nordhorn and also has responsibilities for range control and administration at Decimomannu, Sardinia. No. 431 Maintenance Unit at RAF Bruggen is the supply organisation that provides essential back-up services.

The importance of RAF Germany cannot be under estimated. Its motto 'Keepers of the Peace' underlines the deterrent role it maintains and it is accordingly in the forefront of any re-equipment with the most modern and efficient facilities and aircraft. High priority was given to the replacement of the Jaguar and Buccaneer aircraft within the Command by the sophisticated Tornado and No. XV Squadron became the second RAF unit to receive this new aircraft in 1983. Other squadrons including Nos. 16 at Laarbruch and 14, 17, 20 and 31 at Bruggen have followed. For the time being No. 2 Squadron will remain equipped with Jaguars in the strike/reconnaissance role but will eventually receive Tornado, possibly in 1987.

Right: Loading cluster area-denial bombs onto a Harrier's underwing stations whilst in the field can be a muddy job especially during winter. Members of this ground crew are using blue-painted inert exercise bombs, but it's no less of a difficult job for all that, when one has to be fully kitted up with NBC clothing and gas masks in order to get the job done and at the same time be ready for any emergency.
Below: The Harrier in its element. This No. 4 Squadron aircraft is flying close to the minimum height of 250 feet above ground level allowed over Germany.

RAF Germany's potential as a hard hitting strike force is now being demonstrated in frequent working up exercises designed to get the maximum usefulness out of the Tornado's highly accurate navigation and weapon delivery systems. Deployments to both Red Flag and Maple Flag exercises in the United States and Canada are scheduled to become yearly standing requirements allowing the Tornado to fly over terrain similar to that which it might encounter over the central European front at heights more suitable for operational reasons and not permitted over Germany.

RAF Germany's two air defence squadrons, Nos. 19 and 92, based at Wildenrath and equipped with Phantom FGR.2s, are the only ones fully committed to NATO during peace time. There is a very good reason for this as it is their responsibility to guard against intruders into the Air Defence Identification Zone (ADIZ) a strip of territory along the East-West German borders where intruders have to be recognised and intercepted in minutes of the incident occurring. By Phantom speed the East German border is but 19 minutes flying time away from Wildenrath and Combat Air Patrols are flown while other aircraft from each of the NATO air forces within 2 and 4 ATAF maintain fighter aircraft at immediate readiness to counter any intrusion. These activities are controlled by two Sector Operations Centres.

Each of the Clutch airfields is guarded by an RAF Regiment squadron with Rapier low-level air defence missiles. The largest of these is No. 63 Squadron RAF Regiment, which also deploys into the field with the Harrier force.

Right: No. XV Squadron was the first to receive the Tornado in RAF Germany.
Below: The only RAF Germany squadron still using the Jaguar is No. 2 based at Laarbruch and tasked with photo-reconnaissance duties. This picture was taken at the time No. 2 exchanged its Phantoms for Jaguars in the early seventies. Note the centre-line reconnaissance pack that no No. 2 Squadron Jaguar would be seen without.

Each of the Clutch Stations is now fully equipped with Hardened Aircraft Shelters in which all aircraft are housed when not flying. Each HAS, as mentioned earlier in the chapter on Strike Command, has full facilities to refuel, rearm and service the aircraft; engines can be run inside the building and it is semi-protected against NBC warfare. Each HAS can withstand air attack and they are usually dispersed among the heavily wooded country-side that borders most of the airfields.

One of the tasks of RAF Germany in addition to the strike/attack role is that of close support for the Army in the field. Although BAOR has a large complement of its own battlefield helicopters, the heavy lift and troop rein-forcement roles have traditionally been left to the RAF and for this purpose No. 18 Squadron's Chinooks and No. 230's Pumas provide the means.

Although based at Gutersloh, close to the East-West German border and some distance from the other three

Clutch airfields to the west of the Ruhr, this Station is in the heartland of the British Army dispositions in Germany. The helicopter squadrons are almost always engaged in some exercise or other with the Army and several times a year take part in major manoeuvres plus important operations such as Exercises Crusader and Lionheart in recent times during which the transition to war period was enacted with major troop movements from the United States and the UK supplementing BAOR and other NATO resources.

RAF Germany's Harrier force, consisting of Nos. 3 and 4 Squadrons, is also based at Gutersloh tasked with close support operations for the Army. Their VTOL capa-bilities make them ideal aircraft to position close to the front line where immediate reaction to enemy advances can be countered by concentrated fire power from the air. As with the helicopter force, the Harriers are frequently deployed in the field under the most arduous conditions of weather and environment. Hidden deep inside woods, and using a field not much larger than a football pitch, these squadrons are completely self contained as far as armament and fuel are concerned but because of possible continuous movement during wartime will have to be resupplied by helicopter and ground transport after a period in action. Using the art of camouflage to the full and taking advantage of the terrain, fully loaded Harriers usually use short take-off runs to get airborne with the maximum bomb or rocket load but frequently use their vertical landing abilities on the return to base. Special landing mats are provided for the purpose, often laid by their Army colleagues. Co-operation between the RAF and Army as a completely integrated force can be seen to best advantage under these conditions.

Gutersloh as a base also has another role in time of war namely as the air head for the reinforcement by air of I (Br) Corps from the UK. The rapid movement of troops from reserves held in Britain will be essential if an attack is seriously threatened and transport aircraft from Strike Command, supplemented by civil airliners requisitioned at a moments notice from scheduled service, will be used for this purpose. Exercises Crusader and Lionheart, mentioned earlier, were used in recent years to practise this facility and several thousand troops were quickly transported to their pre-determined positions through the terminal facilities at this vital airfield.

Each of the Clutch airfields has limited resources for air

head operations but during peace time most regular movements by air go through the terminal at RAF Wildenrath mainly because of its closeness to air headquarters at Rheindahlen with Bruggen and Laarbruch not many miles away. Britannia Airways has for many years operated on a contract basis for British Forces in Germany by flying regular trooping flights to Wildenrath on a daily basis. Boeing 737s of this airline are part of the scene taking troops and service families to and from their postings from Luton airport in the UK.

Wildenrath also houses RAF Germany's own miniairline. No. 60 Squadron has operated seven Pembroke C.1 communications aircraft for many years occupying the hangar next to the air terminal at this station. Apart from passenger transport of a VIP nature they also ferry supplies to the other airfields when these are needed in a hurry and are often present at airfields like Northolt near London, collecting or setting down passengers or spare parts for the German squadrons. The Pembroke is long overdue for replacement but no really suitable aircraft can be found to do the work so with their main spars rebuilt it looks as if they may go on providing the essential service they do for a few years to come.

Although RAF Germany operates as a completely independent Command within the Royal Air Force having everything from its own civilian schools for the children of dependants to engineering and maintenance facilities, it is interesting to note that in terms of numbers it has on strength approximately one third of all the operational front line aircraft available in the RAF but only about one ninth of the total manpower, or in other words some 8,000 servicemen stationed there. The effectiveness of this ratio of manpower to operational efficiency is a tribute to the organisation of the Command.

Below: The Saint figure and the crossed keys are the two symbols used by the Tornados of No. 16 Squadron to identify their aircraft. ZA467:FF is seen outside its HAS at Laarbruch.

A five-pointed star on the fin and a
yellow and green chevron on the nose
indicate a No. 31 Squadron Tornado
based at Bruggen.

No. XV Squadron has one of the
simplest unit identification marks of all
RAF Germany Tornado squadrons in
that the Roman numerals 'XV' are the
only adornment on the fin. Coming in to
land at Laarbruch this aircraft is
serialled ZA459:EL.

One of the most attractive colour
schemes on RAF Germany Tornados
belongs to No. 17 Squadron with a
mailed fist in a shield on the fin and
black and white zigzags on the nose
chevron.

About to be towed into its HAS, this No.
20 Squadron Tornado belongs to one of
the four squadrons using this type at
Bruggen. Note the copious amounts of
barbed wire protecting the security area
surrounding the dispersals.

Left: A Puma HC.1 of No. 230 Squadron air lifting a Land Rover trailer for the Army during Exercise Lionheart in July 1984. These aircraft are equally adaptable to carry anything up to a vehicle the size of a Land Rover rapidly over difficult country where troops can best deploy to meet any attack.

Above: Chinooks and Pumas from RAF Gutersloh were fully committed during Exercise Lionheart. Here platoons of British infantry are emplaning from camouflaged positions on the edge of wooded terrain for rapid field deployment elsewhere. Each Chinook can carry up to 44 fully-equipped troops on each sortie over short distances. Mobility in the field can be of tremendous importance to an Army commander faced with difficult deployment decisions in the face of a threatened attack by a numerically superior enemy.

Right: Although designed to be completely independent of a fixed base, RAF Germany's Harrier force has to be re-supplied with weapons and fuel. In this picture an RAF truck has arrived at one of the Harrier hides and its load of bombs is quickly being off-loaded and transported into the less exposed bomb dump which is camouflaged deep in the woodland.

Above: The Chinook can carry loads up to 28,000 pounds on triple hooks under the fuselage. In this picture a No. 18 Squadron aircraft is hovering in preparation to lift a Land Rover and a large quantity of stores during Exercise Lionheart. Note the legs of the crewman seated on the entrance door coaming, on the starboard side, directing operations for the pilot whose visibility is somewhat restricted at this stage.

Left: The RAF Regiment in Germany has a squadron of Scorpion tanks permanently based alongside the Harriers at Gutersloh. Armed with a 76-mm gun these fast, hard hitting, AFVs deploy with the aircraft to guard the hides against surprise attack.

Above: High above the Mediterranean this No. 92 Squadron Phantom FGR.2 from RAF Germany manoeuvres into an attacking position for air-to-air firing against the sleeve target towed by a No. 100 Squadron Canberra while on armament practice camp in Cyprus.
Below: Servicing the Vulcan cannon mounted on the centre line of a No. 92 Squadron Phantom FGR.2 at Akrotiri, in between sorties over the range.

Below: Preparing the 20-mm ammunition for the Phantom's SUU 23 Vulcan rotary cannon during an armament practice camp in Cyprus. Each round is tipped with a different colour to identify an individual pilot's scores.

Below: This interesting picture, taken from the rear seat of a Jaguar T.2 illustrates what it looks like to be flying at low-level in a present day front line jet aircraft. The green lines and figures in the centre of the screen are the indications of flight attitude and armament release point shown by the head-up display projected onto a glass screen, rather like a gun sight, in each cockpit.

Two non-operational aircraft which have given long and meritorious service in RAF Germany.

Above: A Hunting Percival Pembroke C.1 of No. 60 Squadron. Based at RAF Wildenrath and responsible for VIP passenger flights and light freight operations, the Pembrokes, seven of which are still flying, have been re-sparred to extend their useful lives as there are few other aircraft that can fill their role so effectively. Although slow and rather noisy, the Pembrokes fly all over Europe and frequently visit the UK carrying out their mundane but essential task.

Right: Maintaining the right to operate aircraft from RAF Gatow in the British Zone of Berlin two DH Chipmunk T.Mk. 10s are the only aircraft permanently based there. One of these, XZ862, is seen here flying over the Havel Lake where once Sunderlands landed during the Berlin airlift in 1948. The Chipmunks patrol the borders of British airspace over Berlin keeping a sharp eye on Soviet activities and at the same time provide at least some air experience flying for the pilots posted to other ground-based jobs in the city. The three air lanes established from West Germany at the time of the Berlin airlift are still maintained and a Berlin Air Safety centre manned by British, American, French and Soviet air traffic controllers guides aircraft along them on scheduled or service flights into the city's three airports.

ROYAL AIR FORCE
SUPPORT
COMMAND

RAF Support Command was originally formed in September 1973 by the merging of Maintenance Command and No. 90 (Signals) Group. During 1977 a further rationalisation took place and Training Command was also incorporated to create the present day Command with its headquarters at RAF Brampton, Huntingdonshire.

As its name implies, Support Command provides the necessary back-up to the two front-line Commands including that of training aircrew and ground tradesmen in their operational tasks. Apart from that, the operation of the Defence Communications Network and other unspecified communications tasks, electrical and aircraft engineering are part of the Command's work. These tasks are concentrated at the various Maintenance Units with the larger ones dealing with the refurbishment of actual aircraft and others specialising in the supply of clothing of all sorts, motor transport and a great variety of miscellaneous items sometimes on a triservice basis for the Army and Navy as well.

All of the RAF's medical services, hospitals and specialist organisations unique to aviation come under Support Command. The Institute of Aviation Medicine, renowned throughout the world, and based at Farnborough, where doctors research the special effects that flying has on the human mind and body, is one of these.

But it is with the pure training side of its operations that Support Command is better known. Starting with the many recruiting offices in major towns and cities in the United Kingdom a young man or woman can enlist for a very worthwhile career in the RAF at the age of 16½ years, possibly after having spent up to three years in the Air Cadet organisation, yet another Support Command responsibility.

RAF apprenticeships, the backbone of the future RAF NCO tradesmen grades are a worthwhile course for entry into a career and these young men go to either Halton, St. Athan, Cosford or Locking after having done a six week basic course at RAF Swinderby in which they learn their left foot from the right with a liberal amount of square bashing. WRAF recruits go to Hereford for their recruit training. Apprentices and direct entry ground tradesmen then go to one of the four Schools of Technical Training for courses varying greatly in length but dominated by the engineering trades. Courses not carried out by the SoTT vary from motor transport work through the School of Music to the Chaplain's School and these are scattered around the permanent RAF Stations mostly in the southern half of the country from the most northerly, namely the Fire Fighting and Safety School at Catterick to the Officers and Aircrew Selection Centre at Biggin Hill, near London.

Previous page: 'Ladies and gentlemen, the Royal Air Force's aerobatic team, the Red Arrows!' is the announcer's remark at the beginning of any of the many shows that the team gives each year during the summer season. Nine British Aerospace Hawk T.Mk. 1s scream overhead and every pair of eyes on the airfield follows their different manoeuvres for the next 15 minutes.

Right: Portrait of a pilot and his aircraft. This self-portrait taken by the rear-seat instructor in a No. 4 FTS Hawk also has the wing man in the picture. The pattern traced on the canopy hood is the explosive wire which detonates a fraction of a second before the ejector seat is fired and is designed to make the pilot's passage through the perspex somewhat easier.

It is the latter which possibly demands most attention for through the hands of the small team of RAF Officers responsible for arranging the three-day series of interviews and aptitude tests pass hundreds of young men wishing to fly at the government's expense. Not many get their wish and those that do find a long and harrowing two years ahead of them before they are able to join an operational squadron in Strike Command or RAF Germany. Obviously, as its name suggests, O & ASC, Biggin Hill is not only responsible for pilot selection but other aircrew grades, the most important of which is that of navigator. Additionally the Selection Centre also caters for the needs of the Royal Navy and Army who need pilots and navigators for either the Fleet Air Arm or Army Air Corps.

The aspirant pilots like their ground trade colleagues go initially to a basic training course. All future officers who pass the Biggin Hill Selection Board report to the Royal Air Force College, Cranwell where for 18 weeks they are given their share of square bashing but also learn the responsibilities of becoming an officer in the RAF. This course is laughingly called the 'knife and fork' course as it is sometimes necessary to teach otherwise worthy entrants the Service way of doing things.

It is from here that the various ground, air, male and female entrants go their separate ways. For the pilots a quick visit to the Aeromedical Training Centre at North

Luffenham gets them fitted with flying clothing and they are lectured on the use of safety equipment and go through the decompression chamber. Only then does their flying begin for the next stage is at RAF Swinderby where for six weeks they fly with the Flying Selection Squadron to establish whether, through no fault of their own, they might have some hitherto unknown deterrent to completing successfully the full flying training course. Consistent air sickness can sometimes be considered a reason for a candidate not being allowed to continue. Those entrants for pilot training who have gained a private licence during their service with the Air Cadets or who have been members of their University Air Squadron miss the Swinderby part of the training and continue at Cranwell on the Jet Provost. The others go to either No. 1 Flying Training School at Linton-on-Ouse or No. 7 FTS Church Fenton. All of them go through a basic course of 93 flying hours in 37 weeks at which point their instructors make a selection and, although the student does have an opportunity to state a preference, he is generally guided by his mentors into becoming either a fast jet, multi-engined or helicopter pilot. Further Jet Provost training for the first two then takes place, varying in the number of hours flown, before more advanced training on the Hawk for the fast jet and the twin-engined Jetstream for the multi-engined student. Helicopter pilots do no more fixed wing flying, instead they go direct to Shawbury and No. 2 FTS to fly the Gazelle. This is followed by advanced training on the Wessex so that by the end of this period they are awarded their wings.

The fast jet pilots then pass out of the direct control of Support Command as they continue with Strike Command's Tactical Weapons Unit to learn their operational trade.

After completing their Initial Officer Training navigators go to No. 6 FTS, Finningley. Their course lasts 14 months and during that time they train in both high and low-level navigation on either the Dominie or Jet Provost learning military as well as civil procedures, radio aids and a small amount of astro-navigation, an art that has no great value with present day navaids available, but could be of infinite use in wartime when most of these may no longer exist.

Finningley also houses training schools for Air Engineers and Air Electronics Officers. These aircrew members join the RAF as sergeants and do a six-week initial training course rather similar to that undertaken by the officers at Cranwell. During their training they spend a lot of time in simulators and on practical flying exercises accompany the student navigators in the Dominie. In each case the course lasts just over a year. The last aircrew category, that of Air Loadmaster uses the Air Loadmaster and School of Parachute Training at Brize Norton for their course.

Flying training is not confined to new students going through the course for the first time. It is often necessary for a pilot to have to 'fly a desk' for a number of years during his career and, depending on the time away from active aviation, he will either go to a refresher flying course or to an Operational Conversion Unit to pick up where he left off.

One has also to remember that instructors have to be instructed. The Central Flying School at RAF Scampton is one of the oldest established formations in British military aviation having links going back before World War 1. Its main function is to produce high quality flying instructors and at the same time maintain standards throughout the flying training syllabus within the Royal Air Force. Although Jet Provost and Bulldog instruction takes place at Scampton the CFS believes that it is important for the instructor trainees to work in an environment in which they will carry on flying once having passed the course. There are CFS detachments at both Shawbury for helicopter training and RAF Valley for fixed wing flying on the BAe Hawk. A trainee instructor will qualify on one type of aircraft and then be posted to either of the Flying Training Schools for a period of about two and a half years before returning to operational flying with a front line squadron. Sometimes, however, instructors so like the job

Below: After completing the FSS selection course at Swinderby, student pilots are subjected to the rigours of the main flying training syllabus at either No. 1 or No. 7 FTS. Their flying is conducted on the Jet Provost T.Mk. 3A on a 37 week course. In this picture a Church Fenton JP is being refuelled between sorties.

and are considered ideal for it, that they do not venture far outside the confines of Support Command. It has also been known for especially suited initial course students to have been given the CFS course immediately after getting their wings and remain in Support Command training others.

The RAF Aerobatic Team, the Red Arrows is also part of the Central Flying School and the team's pilots are all Qualified Flying Instructors (QFIs) before being selected as part of this unique formation. Based at Scampton and flying the BAe Hawk they perform many wonderful aerobatic demonstrations during the summer season.

Aircraft are complicated pieces of mechanical, electrical and hydraulic machinery and it needs a highly trained and specialised force to maintain them and do this task under difficult conditions in peace and war.

All RAF aircraft have, during their life cycles, to go into a central maintenance organisation for major servicing, rectification, modification and reconditioning. Tried and tested schedules based on safety requirements detail when this must be done and an aircraft must come off line at some operational squadron to go back through the maintenance system before appearing some time later as an almost new aircraft depending on what is required on the schedule.

RAF Support Command has two major Aircraft Engineering Units at St. Athan, South Wales and Abingdon, Oxfordshire. The larger of the two is at St. Athan and here there are two wings, one for general engineering work

and the other for aircraft servicing. The former is the larger of the two and is also responsible for deep servicing on the Spey, RB199 and Adour engines used on the aircraft being refurbished by the airframe section. Although major changes to an aircraft type such as the conversion of Nimrod MR.1s into AEW.3s involve their return to the aircraft manufacturer, other items which include changes in aircraft designation such as the modifications required

Right: The Scottish Aviation Bulldog is used almost exclusively by the University Air Squadrons of which there are 15. In this picture the Bulldogs of the Cambridge UAS, with their tail codes conveniently spelling out 'CUAS', fly line abreast for the camera.

Below: A No. 7 FTS Jet Provost during formation flying training, as seen from its wingman.

to Hunters to convert them from Mk. 6 to Mk. 6A, may be done at St. Athan.

A section of the Abingdon organisation, which is unique, is the Field Repair Squadron which is responsible for salvaging crashed aircraft and those damaged through accident or in battle. Specialist techniques have been developed for this work which have been adopted throughout the RAF based on experiments undertaken at Abingdon. On other occasions the Field Repair Squadron sends teams of engineering specialists to stations to undertake maintenance work beyond the day-to-day capabilities of the front-line specialists. A case in point is the work now going on at Lossiemouth with the deep servicing of No. 8 Squadron's Shackletons which have to be kept airworthy until the Nimrod AEW.3 enters service.

Other Supply and Maintenance Units provide essential servicing for aircraft instruments, avionics, flying safety equipment and so on. Delicate work in checking and refurbishing some of these items takes place in special clean room workshops before each item is returned to store ready for re-issue when required.

But apart from the foremost task of keeping aircraft flying, the maintenance side of Support Command looks after the more mundane equipment ranging from typewriters to dental equipment.

The need for rapid, secure, communications within NATO and its subordinate commands has a high priority in the list of requirements in time of war. With the RAF's use of Skynet, the communications satellite, and the complicated series of ground stations using everything from high frequency transmitters to teleprinters and computer controlled automatic message routeing equipment, a large part of the work of Support Command is devoted to keeping these items serviceable and trouble free. The additional responsibility of the radar and electronic countermeasures facilities available is part of this work and the Command advises other Ministry of Defence branches and Allied air forces on all aspects of servicing and operation in this specialist field.

Apart from looking after the actual hardware involved, the communications section of Support Command is responsible for the care and maintenance of the many radar and radio aerials around the world which come under RAF jurisdiction. There is a specialist trade of aerial erector, in which a small group of RAF tradesmen with a head for heights are trained at RAF Digby, Lincolnshire, and carry out their work in all weathers looking down on the world from anything up to 600 feet above ground level.

To ensure that the RAF gets the equipment it wants where it wants it, a highly sophisticated computer controlled system exists which works with precision from a number of centralised depots. Items such as aircraft fuel, ammunition and weapons have top priority but when it is known that the supply organisation has, at any one time, something like one million separate items on charge it can be seen what a complicated operation this can be.

There are three large equipment supply depots in the RAF based at Stafford, Carlisle and Quedgeley but many smaller units such as the Aeronautical Information and Documents Unit at Northolt, for example, looking after maps and airfield information for pilots, has but a few personnel doing this unique job. The supply control centre at what remains of RAF Hendon was once the base for this activity but this has been in the progress of moving away from central London recently.

RAF Support Command has an annual budget in excess of £500 million. In total it embraces 53 major units and 136 smaller ones. In terms of manpower the Command employs some 49,000 people, 14,000 of whom are civilians. At any one time the combined air and ground crew training programme has some 6–8,000 trainees passing through the system though this varies according to the demands made upon the Command by the other two. For a long time, for example, multi-engined pilot training was suspended altogether and the Jetstream T.1s sold as surplus to requirements. Another variable number is the aircraft strength of the Command. At the present time there are about 500 aircraft in the training system, undergoing maintenance in the various MUs or held in storage.

These are quite fantastic figures when one realises that the Royal Air Force today, although improved in efficiency hundreds of times, is very small in terms of aircraft numbers and personnel to what it was 25 years ago. The use of sophisticated techniques and machinery has made up this efficiency and naturally will be developed further as the Service embraces new techniques and disciplines.

Right: Multi-engine students go to RAF Finningley to continue their training after the initial Jet Provost flying. The aircraft used is the Jetstream T.Mk. 1 which has two Astazou turboprops to contend with. It is an ideal aircraft for the purpose and students are introduced to elementary route flying as well as the basic handling of the aircraft.

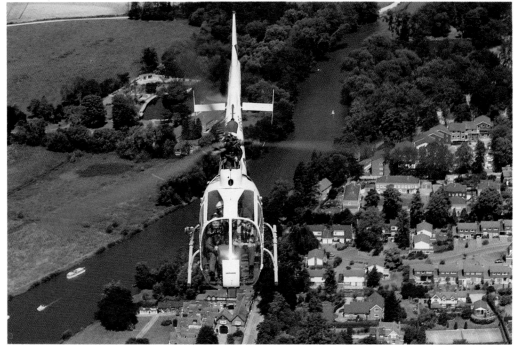

Above: The transition from fixed to rotary winged flight can cause some severe problems for student pilots. The basic course is in the spritely Westland Gazelle and includes, apart from elementary handling exercises, the problems of getting the aircraft in and out of confined spaces. This Gazelle is manoeuvering close to a tree line and discovering the effects of downdraught and what can be done under these conditions.

Left: Gazelle flying has its moments. The student and instructor in this aircraft are obviously enjoying the delights of low flying over the countryside around No. 2 FTS, Shawbury.

Above: The Westland Wessex has largely been superseded in front line squadrons and many of these aircraft have been made available to Support Command for training purposes. No. 2 FTS, Shawbury, uses them exclusively for advanced training covering a 12 week period before the student gains his wings. In this instance the Wessex is negotiating the 'hole in the wood', a series of manoeuvres based on precision flying in which the student has to be able to get his aircraft in and out of a very confined space between 80 ft high trees without help from a crewman conveniently directing his approach.

Left: Get back on the centre line! This Jet Provost, fairly obviously under student control, seems to be wavering away from the runway centre at RAF Dishforth which is used for circuit and landing training. Students spend a lot of time in getting their techniques polished to such an extent that they can, in spite of cross winds put the aircraft down in an attitude which does not give the instructor cause for alarm.

Above: The BAe Dominie is used for both navigator and aircrew engineer training. Based at Finningley the students do long cross country flights and before the end of the course have to do a maximum of two overseas sorties to either Berlin or Gibraltar during which the navigation has to be according to the book as far as civil flight procedures are concerned. During the 20 years that the Dominie has been in RAF service there have been no major accidents involving this type and their safety record has been second to none.

Below: Round again Hoskins! This Jetstream is engaged in circuits and landings in order that the student pilot thoroughly masters the complicated and sometimes frightening occurrences of engine failure during this sort of manoeuvre. Once over the initial problems of handling the aircraft on straightforward landings the instructor will apply any number of different problems for the student to cope with including perhaps engine failure, fire on board or electronics malfunction during the approach to landing or take-off.

Left: These five illustrations show what the best dressed air crew are wearing these days. On the left is the basic overall with an umbilical cord for connecting to the aircraft's systems. Next comes an immersion suit so that protection is given in the event of ditching in the sea. Flying overalls and the life jacket are next added followed by a bone dome with its attendant face mask and oxygen system. Finally an independent life support system is added so that aircrew members can board their aircraft under NCB conditions without recourse to gas masks and other protective clothing.

Left: One of Support Command's aerobatic team, the Red Arrows seen at one of the major biennial displays at the SBAC show, Farnborough.

Right: A student pilot is instructed in the correct procedure in positioning himself in the cockpit of a Hawk T.1 shortly after arriving at RAF Valley for the more advanced flying training course which those selected for fast jet training have to undergo. An interesting observation at this point is that the student's flying clothing knee pads have the words 'left' and 'right' written as appropriate. Surely that sort of elementary knowledge does not need to be taught at this stage!

Although aircrew rarely like to mention it, there is an absolute need for efficient fire fighting services at all RAF airfields. Ground crews specialising in this trade are given the most thorough training at RAF Catterick and have, during their 25 week course, to practise the most efficient ways in which to tackle an aircraft fire after a crash and the extrication of trapped aircrew. These two pictures taken at Catterick show members of RAF fire fighting teams under training (*left*) in the best way in which to get into an aircraft on fire and (*above*) the use of foam extinguishers to subdue aircraft fuel fires. The most modern techniques are used by RAF fire fighting crews and at almost every airfield an old airframe, surplus to requirements, is positioned so that they can keep up-to-date on methods which all aircrew sincerely hope will never have to be used. Regular practice is needed to ensure the right combination of efficiency and speed.

Right: So that's how it works Chiefy!
The goggle-eyed airman on the left is
obviously impressed by the instructor
showing him the many blades that make
up the internal components of the
modern day jet engine's compressor.
This sectionalised engine at the School
of Technical Training, RAF Halton is
just one small part of the many training
aids used by trade training instructors in
Support Command today. Ground crew
training is both efficient and thorough in
spite of the constant demands and
changes made by technological advances
in aero engine development.

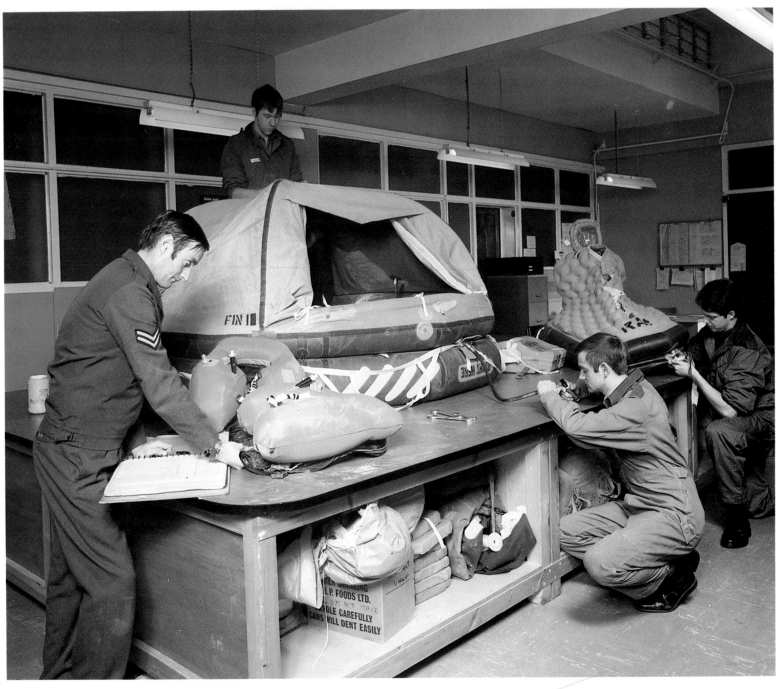

Left: If there was ever a need for an aircraft to ditch in the sea the crew on board would need the services of their Station's safety equipment section. Constant maintenance of personal life jackets, individual aircrew dinghies and as shown in the background to this picture, five-man life rafts, has to be on the top line. The safety equipment section at any operational or training airfield has an arduous task in making sure that no possible failure can occur in the life-saving equipment under their charge.

Above: Trade training in the catering branch is no less thorough than in any of the more popular trades which may from time to time come into the limelight. Here, trainees are setting up a field kitchen simulating operations in one of the more remote parts of the world where no normal services are available and hot meals and drinks have to be in constant supply due to the operational requirements of the unit to which the airmen responsible are attached. Their fully mobile kitchens are much appreciated by ground and aircrew alike under the arduous conditions that often prevail when operating under close

surveillance by the enemy and where environmental conditions make it almost impossible to provide a 'char and wad' for those closely engaged in the battle. In spite of having to maintain a low profile with camouflage netting hiding their activities the largely unsung attributes of the RAF's 'cooks and bottle-washers' are more valued than even they would care to admit.

RESEARCH AND DEVELOPMENT

Although the work of today's Royal Air Force can be described under three separate headings corresponding to the main Commands, Strike, Support and RAF Germany, there are a number of other, smaller units that do not necessarily fit into this pattern or which come under the Ministry of Defence (Procurement Executive) whose aircraft fleet is manned by Royal Air Force aircrew even though the ground servicing is in civilian hands.

In producing the final chapter in this book, therefore, an attempt has been made to tidy up and give a look into the future as far as new aircraft and the next generation of equipment is concerned.

One of the most interesting and varied fleets of aircraft on the periphery of the RAF is that operated by the research establishments. Of these the most important is the Royal Aircraft Establishment, Farnborough, known to thousands as the venue of the bi-annual Society of British Aerospace Companies exhibition and flying display. Its daily work, however, concerns many aspects of research into aircraft structures, missiles, avionics and a host of allied subjects. Together with the outstations at Bedford, Aberporth, Llanbedr and West Freugh, the RAE has a varied selection of aircraft ranging from a Tornado to a BAC One Eleven.

The Institute of Aviation Medicine also at Farnborough is a separate establishment at which research is conducted into human reactions to the aviation environment.

At Boscombe Down the Aeroplane and Armament Experimental Establishment is responsible for testing pre-service aircraft and equipment be it a new weapons system or an electronic prototype requiring Service acceptance before going into production. A separate unit was formed within A & AEE, for example, to cover the tremendous amount of work involved in getting Tornado into squadron use. The Empire Test Pilots School is also based at Boscombe Down and here test pilots from all three Services plus those from overseas are trained.

The Royal Radar Establishment at Malvern, Worcs, as its name implies, is concerned with both ground and airborne radars and uses some of the aircraft at Bedford for experimental work now that its own airfield at Pershore has been closed.

The Royal Air Force, in looking to the future, is awaiting delivery of the fighter version of the Tornado to frontline squadrons, the advent of the Nimrod AEW.3 and the Harrier GR.5 and the introduction of the Shorts Tucano to replace the Jet Provost as the basic training aircraft. In the 1990s a new fighter will have to be developed and already prototypes are beginning to appear. The RAF faces the next ten years as an almost total Tornado force for both strike and defence. With the advent of the new Harrier GR.5 this should present a formidable deterrent.

Previous page: The only Lockheed Hercules W.2 is operated by the Meteorological Research Flight at Farnborough. Its long nose probe and cockpit-mounted radome give it a distinctive appearance. Serialled XV208, this aircraft goes looking for hurricanes, typhoons and other weather phenomena such as clear air turbulence and windsheer, all matters of great concern to aviators. From the measurements and data gained on these flights, scientific staff are able to discover patterns and plot where weather conditions of an extreme nature arise so that better predictions can be issued on the strength of these findings.

Right: Pilotless target drones are operated by RAF Llanbedr for use over the Aberporth ranges off the Welsh coast. Both ground-to-air and air-to-air missiles are fired against them and sensitive cameras and miss-distance recorders check the accuracy from the target itself. This Meteor U.8 is one of the few still remaining of this type and has the pilotless target's distinctive red and yellow colour scheme.

Left: The Empire Test Pilots School at Boscombe Down trains test pilots and observers for work in the research establishments themselves and often in industry. All three Services and overseas countries contribute suitable students for the year-long course which uses a variety of aircraft from the ETPS fleet and also borrows others from A & AEE. In this instance the BAe Hawk T.1, XX343, is a dedicated ETPS aircraft and ideally suited for the work involved. It is one of three in use which have had modifications such as different instrumentation fitted. One of the Hawks has also been modified as a variable stability aircraft to train students in this aspect of test flying.

Due to fly in the later part of 1986 the British Aerospace Experimental Aircraft Programme demonstrator will be powered by two RB.199 turbofans and used to establish the requirements for the next generation of fighter aircraft for Britain, and possibly other countries within NATO, following agreement reached in mid 1985. It is in direct competition with the French Rafale prototype also built for the same purpose though the French have opted out of the main European programme. Many advanced technology ideas and new aerodynamic features will be built into these aircraft since it is necessary to establish flight parameters before final commitment to a design is made because, with the large amounts of money needed in the design and development stages, governments have to be certain of what they are getting before orders are placed. These two pictures show what the EAP will look like. The inset was taken in 1985 when the aircraft was half way through its construction at Warton.

Three Canberras in the MoD (PE) fleet.
Left top: WV787 is a converted B(I)8 which is used to spray water onto an aircraft following immediately astern to simulate ice formation.
Left centre: Looking like an ordinary Canberra B.6, WK163, is based at RAE Bedford. The nature of its duties is classified but the close observer will note an unusual bulge under the centre section where once the bomb bay used to be.
Left bottom: When the Royal Radar Establishment gave up its airfield at Pershore, flying activities necessary to test airborne radar equipment were moved to RAE Bedford. Canberra B.6 WH953, with a large radome in the nose, is one of the aircraft used for this purpose.

Mention should be made of the MoD (PE) aircraft fleet's special colour scheme in which most of the aircraft permanently attached are painted. Known as 'raspberry ripple' the distinctive blue, red and white scheme has the advantage of high visibility under different light conditions, a necessary requirement on occasions when the aircraft is performing some complicated manoeuvre at the behest of the scientists operating their equipment in the cabin or rear seat of the aircraft.

Above: Among the former RAF aircraft operated at RAE Farnborough is a civil airliner in the shape of BAC One Eleven Series 402 now serialled XX919. Although it still has limited passenger capabilities the inside of the cabin has been converted into a flying laboratory where experimental equipment can be installed and evaluated by a small team of experts from Farnborough's scientific staff.

Below: RAE Bedford's sole HS.125 XW930 is a former civil aircraft bought for use by the establishment for research into gust response. The interior of the cabin is filled with scientific measuring equipment and the nose fitted with a long probe on the end of which a number of sensitive recording instruments can be fitted.

Left: The political and military controversy surrounding the introduction of the Nimrod AEW.3 into RAF service and the amounts of money being spent on perfecting the sophisticated radar on board, has rarely had such far reaching affects for any other aircraft that the RAF has ever owned. Eleven Nimrod maritime patrol aircraft have been allocated for conversion with the addition of large radar bulges at nose and tail. The trouble has been attributed to the overheating of the equipment when installed on board the Nimrod. By the end of 1985 two Nimrod AEW.3s had been delivered to RAF Waddington, their destined base but the desired operational standard had still not been met. It was pointed out that it could have been possible to buy American AWACS aircraft at a much earlier date and have had them in service sooner and at less cost.

Above: The first British Harrier GR.5 seen at Dunsfold at the time of its roll-out in mid-1985. ZD318 is painted in air superiority grey and much of the construction of the wing is in carbon reinforced plastics, a novel introduction for aircraft applications. British Aerospace and the American manufacturer McDonnell-Douglas have co-operated in the production of the Harrier GR.5, or AV-8B as the US Marine Corps know it. The first production examples were beginning to reach the US Marines by the end of 1985 and the RAF's first examples should be delivered by late 1986. The extra power-to-weight ratio available in this aircraft allows for an additional two underwing weapons strong points as well as a considerable improvement in performance.

Overleaf: The Shorts Tucano T.Mk. 1 has been selected to replace the Jet Provost as the RAF's basic trainer. The new aircraft breaks with a tradition established by the Royal Air Force when the JP first came into service in 1955 for all-through pure-jet training for pilots. It has a turboprop engine and is much smaller than the Jet Provost, employing tandem seating in line with the BAe Hawk onto which students will graduate after their basic flying course. The selection of the Tucano, which was offered in accordance with the requirements of AST412, was made in the face of fierce competition from British Aerospace who put forward the Pilatus PC-9 after over 30 other competing designs had been eliminated. A total of 130 Tucanos has been ordered and the first should be available in early 1987. Short Brothers are also hoping for overseas sales of Tucanos.

93

Just about the oldest aircraft still in RAF markings and active service is Douglas Dakota ZA947 which is part of the MoD (PE) fleet at the Royal Aircraft Establishment, Farnborough. This machine has been used for experimental work for much of its life and, although it is also able to be fitted with passenger seating, performs a number of otherwise important tasks for the establishment. Very much in demand during 1985 for the celebration of the Dakota's 50th anniversary, ZA947 was given a special paint scheme for its participation in the International Air Tattoo held at Fairford in July.

Normally it appears in the raspberry ripple colours as seen here. It was built in 1943 and originally serialled KG661, an error that was not put right until 1979, as a previous RAF Dakota had already been allocated this number years before.